Studies In Jainism:

Primer

Edited by

Duli Chandra Jain

Jain Study Circle

Editorial Advisors:

Vinay K. Vakani	Chandrakant P. Shah	Krishna Kumar Mehta
Jyantilal Shah	Ahamindra Jain	Anil & Parnita Jain
Sunita Jain	Richa Jain, Rashmi Jain	Rajesh Jain

Cover:
Interior views of Delwara Jain Temples
Mt. Abu, Rajasthan, India
Photos by DCJ

Library of Congress Catalog Card No. 90 - 091543

ISBN   0 - 9626105 - 1 - 8   Softcover

Published by
Jain Study Circle, Inc.
99-11 60 Avenue, #3D
Flushing, New York, 11368
USA

Printed in the United States of America

Idol Of A TEERTHANKAR

Dedicated to

The New Generation Of Jains

Contents

Preface

These are exciting times for Jainism. For the first time in recorded history, a significant population of Jains is residing outside of India. We are living in the age of science and technology, computers and communication satellites, and rockets and space exploration. All over the world, political and socio-economic systems are undergoing important changes. With the dawn of freedom and democracy, which some of us have personally witnessed, India has made significant progress in the past few decades in various fields including agriculture, industry and education. Indians who have migrated to North America, including youngsters, have made excellent use of the opportunities presented to them. Jains are no exception.

In India as well as in North America, Jains are playing a significant role in diverse fields and are enjoying the benefits of their endeavors. There has been a significant rise in the level of education in the Jain community. Consequently, Jains have achieved greater awareness and understanding of the basics of religion. They have developed the ability to distinguish between blind faith and rationalism, between myths and reality, and between meaningless rituals and the genuine practice of religion. A healthy dialogue is continuing on the unique features of Jainism. The series 'Studies In Jainism' is an effort to contribute to this dialogue.

The concepts presented in the book conform to the Jain scriptures, which are works of great thinkers and philosophers of the past. Every effort has been made to avoid views and interpretations of scriptures given by individual preachers and writers.

The code of ethics of all religions including Jainism, is essentially the same. However, the Jain code of conduct is based on our concepts of universe and of reality. Moreover, Jains practice ethical conduct not because some higher authority commands them to do so. They do not celebrate any worship to please any superhuman or supernatural being. Jains conduct their lives in a rational manner in order to attain happiness and peace of mind individually as well as collectively.

The present book is part of the series: Studies In Jainism: Reader 1 and Reader 2. It is the result of the joint effort of a large group of individuals. Most of the material has been adopted from the Jain Study Circular. Thus, the writers of the Jain Study Circular should be given the most credit for their contributions. The editorial advisors have made valuable comments and suggestions. I am also grateful for the advice, encouragement and help given by Ms. Kristin Dervishian, Dr. Jyotiben Gandhi, Dr. Chaman Lal Jain, Mr. Shital Prasad Jain, Dr. T. J. Salgia, Mr. Naresh Shah and other friends.

D. C. J.

Guru, Father and Mother

"The Acharya", we read in the VASHISHTHA SMRITI, "is ten times more honorable than an UPAADHYAAYA; the father a hundred times more than the Acharya, and the mother a thousand times more than the father."

- The Legacy of India, page 147
Oxford University Press, 1962

NAMOKAAR MANTRA
(Reverence Mantra)

NAMO ARIHANTAANAM

We revere ARIHANTS, the Supreme Human Beings.
ARIHANTS know the absolute truth.
They devote their lives to uplift life on earth.

NAMO SIDDHAANAM

We revere SIDDHAS, the Supreme Beings.
SIDDHAS are souls having absolute perception, knowledge and bliss.

NAMO AYARIYAANAM

We revere ACHARYAS, the sages who preach.
ACHARYAS master the principles of religion.

NAMO UVAJJHAAYAANAM

We revere UPAADHYAAYAS, the sages who study.
UPAADHYAAYAS study and get knowledge of matter and souls.

NAMO LOAE SAVVA SAAHOONAM

We revere all SADHUS, the sages who fully practice the teachings of religion. SADHUS show us the way to make our lives happy and peaceful.

We worship the virtues of ARIHANTS, SIDDHAS, ACHARYAS, UPAADHYAAYAS and SADHUS to make our lives better.

What is NAMOKAAR MANTRA?

Alpa: Ma, what is NAMOKAAR Mantra?

Ma: Alpa, NAMOKAAR Mantra is a prayer. We pay our respects to the five supreme benevolent personalities (persons most helpful to all, PARAMESHTHI) by reciting NAMOKAAR Mantra.

Alpa: Who are the five supreme benevolent personalities?

Ma: The five supreme benevolent personalities are ARIHANTS, SIDDHAS, ACHARYAS, UPAADHYAAYAS and SADHUS. We can make our lives better by learning their virtues (good qualities). So they are called supreme benevolent personalities.

Neel: Who is an ARIHANT?

Ma: An ARIHANT is a supreme human being who knows the absolute truth. He knows all things. He is omniscient (KEVALI), one who has perfect knowledge.

Alpa: Who are SIDDHAS?

Ma: SIDDHAS are pure souls. They have freed themselves from all kinds of bondage.

Neel: Ma, do SIDDHAS know the absolute truth?

Ma: Yes, SIDDHAS do know the absolute truth. In fact, ARIHANTS become SIDDHAS (pure souls) at the end of their lives. SIDDHAS have a higher spiritual position than ARIHANTS. But we pay our respects to

ARIHANTS first because they are living ideals for us.

Alpa: Who is an ACHARYA?

Ma: An ACHARYA is a monk who teaches the principles of religion.

Neel: Who is an UPAADHYAAYA?

Ma: A monk who studies the principles of religion is called an UPAADHYAAYA.

Alpa: Who is a SADHU?

Ma: A person who fully practices the teachings of religion is a SADHU (monk). SADHUS lead good, peaceful lives. Thus SADHUS present a good example for others.

Neel: What is the difference between ACHARYAS, UPAADHYAAYAS and SADHUS?

Ma: ACHARYAS, UPAADHYAAYAS and SADHUS are all monks. All monks study and practice the teachings of religion. The basic difference between them is that an ACHARYA is the head of a group of monks and UPAADHYAAYAS spend most of their time in studying religious books.

Alpa: Ma, why do we revere the five supreme benevolent personalities in NAMOKAAR Mantra?

Ma: We revere them so that we can learn good things. We keep away from bad thoughts while reciting NAMOKAAR Mantra. We learn to be good by reciting NAMOKAAR Mantra. Thus NAMOKAAR Mantra helps us to make our lives better.

True Identity Of Jains

A True Story

Narrated by Shri Sumer Chand Jain

In the past, Jains were known to speak the truth and avoid violence to all living beings. Even these days, although to a lesser extent, people hold similar views about Jains.

This is a story from the school days of Shri Akshaya Kumar Jain, editor of the prominent Indian daily newspaper, Navabharat Times, and a renowned Jain scholar. One day, two ninth-grade students had an argument and a fight. They were brought before the headmaster (principal) of the school. The two students gave conflicting accounts of the incident. The headmaster could not figure out who was telling the truth. He did not know what to do until someone mentioned that Akshaya Kumar, who was in the seventh grade, had seen the incident. The headmaster said, "Akshaya Kumar belongs to a Jain family. A Jain will certainly speak the truth." So he called Akshaya Kumar to his office. The headmaster got the true story from him and admonished (gave a warning to) the student who was at fault.

It is good to behave like a true Jain.

The Universe

We see the earth, the sky, the sun, the moon and the stars. All these things are part of the universe. People, cows, horses, lions, dogs, cats, worms and insects are part of the universe. Trees and plants, mountains and rivers are also part of the universe.

We see that there are living beings in the universe. We see that there are non-living things in the universe.

The non-living things are:

1. Matter and energy - water, earth, air, heat, light and other similar things
2. Principle of motion - the principle that describes how things move
3. Principle of rest - the principle that describes how things stay at rest
4. Space - the thing where other things reside
5. Time - the thing that helps other things change

These five things are called non-living entities (DRAVYAS).

Living beings are born. They consume food, water and air. They grow on their own while non-living things do not grow on their own. Men, animals, plants and trees are living beings.

Jainism says that each living being has a soul. The body of a living being is made up of matter and energy. A soul lives in the body. Soul is a living entity. There are two kinds of souls in the universe: worldly souls and liberated souls. Worldly souls have bodies. Some fine particles of matter called karmas are also attached to the worldly souls. When a worldly soul is able to remove all karmas, it becomes pure. Such liberated souls are called SIDDHAs.

Thus there are six entities in the universe: souls, matter and energy, principle of motion, principle of rest, space and time. Only matter and energy can be detected by our senses of touch, taste, smell, sight and hearing. The other five entities cannot be detected by our senses.

Matter and energy are useful to all living beings. Jainism says that the function or role of living beings is to help each other. All living beings depend on one another. We need all things in nature to survive. So we should help all living beings. We should avoid hurting living beings. This is the Jain teaching of nonviolence (AHIMSA).

A Boy And A Scorpion

by Kanti Mepani

Raju was a teenager. He had learned the basic teachings of religion at a Jain school. He learned that religion (DHARM) means natural qualities or attributes of a thing or person. Jainism says that, by nature, man has good qualities, like nonviolence, compassion, and helping other living beings. These constitute the religion of a man. Raju learned that nonviolence is the greatest religion. Our belief in nonviolence implies that every living being has the right to live and holds a unique place in nature. Therefore we should not intentionally injure even the insects and animals that may harm us. Raju understood these ideas and practiced them.

One day, Raju's mother took him to a park. She sat on a bench while he played with other children. There was a large mud hole in the park under a tree. Raju saw a scorpion floating in the mud hole. The scorpion was struggling to get out. Raju tried to rescue it but he got stung by the scorpion. The sting was mild. So Raju tried again but failed.

Raju's mother saw this and thought that Raju was playing with the scorpion. She said to Raju, "Leave the scorpion alone. I do not want you to get hurt."

Raju replied, "Ma, I am trying to save this scorpion from drowning."

His mother said, "Keep away from the scorpion. It is the nature of a scorpion to sting when it senses danger."

"Ma, but my nature (DHARM) is to have compassion and to help other living beings. The scorpion does not give up its nature. Why should I?"

With the help of his mother, Raju carefully took the scorpion out of the mud hole and put it on the grass in a remote area of the park. His mother felt very good about her son.

* * * * * * *

The doctrine of nonviolence is not for the weak and the cowardly; it is meant for the brave and the strong. The bravest man allows himself to be killed without killing. And he desists from killing or injuring, because he knows that it is wrong to injure.
— Mahatma Gandhi, in the Magazine 'HARIJAN'
August 17, 1935

* * * * * * *

Our Religion

Anil: Grandma, what is religion?

Grandma: To most people, religion means faith. People believe in things taught by their religion. However, the Sanskrit word for religion has a somewhat different meaning. The Sanskrit word for religion is DHARM. It means nature or qualities of a thing or person.

Asha: Grandma, how can religion mean the qualities of a person? If a man does bad things, can we say it is his religion?

Grandma: Children, the good qualities of a person make up his or her DHARM. We believe that man is good by nature. Doing good things is man's religion. Sometimes, a man does not understand and does bad things by giving up his true nature. This is like giving up one's religion.

Anil: This is an interesting idea. I have heard that the Sanskrit word DHARM has another meaning as well.

Grandma: Yes, the other meaning of the word DHARM is duty. Jainism says that the function (role) of living beings is to help each other. Thus helping each other is our duty (DHARM or religion).

Asha: Grandma, you said that helping each other is our

duty. Being good is our religion. Why is it so?

Grandma: Let me give you a simple example. All parents love their children. All children love their parents. Our mothers and fathers do everything to make our lives comfortable. They help us to become good people. All family members love us and help us. They do not want anything in return. Thus it is our religion to be good to our parents and other family members.

Anil: This is a good idea. But why do we have to be good to other people? Why should we be kind to animals?

Grandma: We do not like to get hurt. We avoid pain. We do not want to die. No living being likes to get hurt. No living being wants to die. Therefore we avoid hurting or killing people, animals and insects. We do not kill animals for food. That is why we Jains are vegetarians. This is our religion of nonviolence (AHIMSA).

Asha: Grandma, please tell us the basic teachings of the Jain religion.

Grandma: The basic teachings of the Jain religion are:
1. Nonviolence (AHIMSA)
   We do not hurt others. We do not speak of hurting others. We do not think of hurting others.
2. Truth (SATYA)
   We always speak the truth.

3. Non-stealing (ACHAURYA)

We do not steal or take things that do not belong to us.

4. Purity of body and mind (BRAHMACHARYA)

We keep our bodies clean and have good thoughts.

5. Non-possessiveness (APARIGRAH)

We do not become selfish. We limit our needs.

Children, remember, truth, non-stealing, purity of body and mind, and non-possessiveness are part of nonviolence.

Other religions have similar teachings.

Asha: I understand why we should not hurt or kill living beings. But why do we have to speak the truth and follow other teachings of Jainism?

Grandma: Our feelings are hurt when someone tells us a lie. We do not like it when someone takes away something that belongs to us. When somebody gets angry at us, we feel hurt. When we become angry, we ourselves get hurt. We are unhappy when someone is selfish and does not care about us. This means that hurting the feelings of others is violence. Hurting our own feelings is also violence. If we want to be happy, we should avoid such violence.

Jainism says that nonviolence is the supreme religion.

Subtle Influence of Nonviolence[1]

Mr. Anderson, an European gentleman, went tiger hunting in the forest of Jayadebpur. He was riding an elephant. On seeing a tiger, the elephant was frightened and Mr. Anderson was thrown off its back. While on the ground, Mr. Anderson fired two or three times at the tiger but missed his aim. So he began to run. The tiger chased him. While running from the tiger, Mr. Anderson sighted a naked monk. The monk showed no panic. So Mr. Anderson went near the monk. The monk asked Mr. Anderson to sit down and, by waving his hand, the monk signaled the tiger to stop. The tiger sat at a distance, wagged his tail, growled for some time and then went away. Mr. Anderson was surprised and asked the monk how he was able to pacify the tiger. The monk replied: You had the intention of killing the tiger and so you were being attacked by him. On the other hand, I remained calm. I did not show any feelings of fear, anger or violence toward the tiger. So the tiger saw no danger and became pacified. In many instances, one who has nonviolent thoughts, speech and actions is not attacked even by wild beasts.

---

1 Adapted from the Introduction, by Ajit Prasad Jain, of Acharya Amrit Chandra Suri's PURUSHAARTH SIDDYUPAAYA, Central Jaina Publishing House, Lucknow, U. P., India, 1933, pages 12-13.

A Prayer To JIN

by Duli Chandra Jain

I pray to JIN – the victor,
who has conquered his desires and passions.
I pray to VEETARAAG,
who is free from likes and dislikes.
I pray to the omniscient KEVALI who is like
a sun that brings out the real nature of things.
I pray to TEERTHANKARS,
who reform the religious system
and reinstate the religious order.

JIN is VEETARAAG;
JIN is omniscient.
TEERTHANKAR is JIN.
JIN becomes free from bondage of matter.
He becomes SIDDHA – a pure liberated soul.

A liberated soul does not indulge
in things and events of the universe.
He does not reward or punish us.

I pray to JIN, not asking for anything,
but with a resolve to attain his virtues.

The Dilemma Of A Liar

by Piyush Golia[1]

Ravi and Shamu were good friends. They were both in the tenth grade. One day Ravi needed a science textbook so he went to Shamu. He said, "Shamu, may I borrow your science textbook? I have to study for tomorrow's test. I will return it to you tomorrow after the test."

Shamu also had to study for the test, so he could not loan Ravi the book. However, he did not want to tell Ravi that he too had to study for the test. He liked to show off that he was doing well in school without any effort. So Shamu said, "Sorry my friend, Lalu has already borrowed my book."

Ravi calmly said, "Never mind. I will go to Lalu and ask him to lend me the book." Ravi started to walk towards Lalu's house.

Shamu had not anticipated this turn of events. He knew that when Ravi reached Lalu's place, the truth would come out. He realized that he was about to lose the trust and respect of his friends and classmates. Everybody would make fun of him. He had no choice

1 Son of Kanak and Prabha Golia

but to get to Lalu's place before Ravi. He took a short cut and ran as fast as he could. On reaching Lalu's house, Shamu said to him, "When Ravi comes and asks you for the science textbook, tell him that you need it yourself to study for the test." Lalu did not understand what was going on but Shamu did not give him a chance to ask any questions. Shamu knew that Ravi was on his way, so he was in a hurry to leave.

As Shamu left, Ravi arrived and asked Lalu if he could borrow the science textbook. Lalu told him that he did not have the book. Now the situation became clear. They both understood what Shamu had done. Lalu also wanted to study for the test. So both Lalu and Ravi went to the library and studied for the test.

Shamu, on the other hand, had the book but he was in no mood to study. The thoughts of shame would not go away. He could not concentrate and study for the test. The more he thought of the test, the more worried he became. The result was obvious. He said to himself, "Why did I put myself in such a miserable position?"

Jains Are Vegetarians

We Jains practice nonviolence. Meat is produced by killing animals, which is gross violence. Therefore, we are vegetarians. We eat food made with grains, vegetables, fruits and milk. Vegetarian food contains all the things that are necessary for healthy living. Further, there is much less violence in producing vegetarian food. Billions of animals are killed for non-vegetarian food every year. In most cases, plants do not have to be killed to obtain vegetarian food.

A comparison of meat-eating animals (carnivores), plant-eating animals (herbivores) and humans shows that man is vegetarian by nature. Thus vegetarian food is more suitable for our bodies.

Carnivores (meat-eating)	Herbivores (plant-eating)	Humans
Have claws for killing	Have no claws	Have no claws
Sharp front teeth for tearing meat	No sharp front teeth	No sharp front teeth
Stomach acid is 20 times stronger	Weak acid in stomach	Weak acid in stomach
Perspire through tongue	Perspire through skin	Perspire through skin

Scientists have found that the high-fat, high-cholesterol and low-fiber content of meat and eggs are linked with cancer of the brain, lungs, liver, stomach, intestines, pancreas and breast. Farm animals are given hormones, tranquilizers, antibiotics and many other drugs and chemicals. Some of these substances may cause cancer and other diseases. On the other hand, grains, lentils, fruits and vegetables contain vitamins and minerals that protect us from diseases. When we get sick by eating unhealthy food, our feelings are hurt. This is violence of self. We avoid such violence by eating healthy vegetarian food.

When we go to the supermarket to shop for food, we need to carefully read the ingredients of the food before buying it. Similarly, when we eat outside, we should carefully avoid food containing eggs, meat and meat products.

Vegetarianism is good for us. It is essential for our practice of nonviolence.

*   *   *   *   *   *   *

The U.S. Surgeon General has reported that 70% of deaths in the United States are related to diet, especially the over-consumption of beef and other saturated fats. Americans now eat 25% of all the beef consumed in the world, a habit that all reputable research has linked to heart disease, colon and breast cancers and strokes.

*   *   *   *   *   *   *

18

 ## Queen Chelna And King Shrenik

This is a story of the times of Bhagwaan Mahaveer.[1] At that time, King Chetak was the chief of the Republic of Vaishali. He had a beautiful daughter named Chelna. An artist painted a portrait of Princess Chelna and took it to King Shrenik, the ruler of Magadh. Charmed by Chelna's beauty, Shrenik fell in love with her. Once Chelna visited Rajgrah, the capital of Magadh. On seeing King Shrenik, she too fell in love with him, and the two were married.

Queen Chelna was devoted to Jainism while King Shrenik followed Buddhism. King Shrenik was intelligent and kind. However, he did not like Chelna's devotion to Jain monks. He believed that no human being could follow the difficult path of Jainism. He thought that the sacrifice and penance of Jain monks were just for show. He wanted to show Chelna that Jain monks were phony.

One day King Shrenik went to a forest. There he saw a Jain monk, Yamadhar, who was engaged in deep meditation. King Shrenik signaled his pet dogs to attack the monk. Yamadhar remained calm and quiet. So the dogs too became pacified. King Shrenik was

1 The word 'Bhagwaan' means virtuous and respectable.

surprised. He thought that Yamadhar must have played some trick. He became very angry and started shooting arrows towards the monk. Being very upset, King Shrenik kept on missing his aim. At last, he put a dead snake around Yamadhar's neck and returned to his palace.

King Shrenik related the whole story to Queen Chelna. The queen felt very sad and took Shrenik back to Yamadhar. The monk was still in meditation. Because of the dead snake, ants were crawling all over the monk's body. Shrenik was very much surprised to see that Yamadhar had remained calm and peaceful. Chelna felt sorry to see what Shrenik had done. The king and queen gently removed the dead snake and ants from the monk's body. Yamadhar opened his eyes and blessed the king and queen. He was not angry with Shrenik. King Shrenik was greatly impressed by this example of tolerance and calmness. He understood that Jain monks do not have likes and dislikes. They treat both friend and foe alike. They are VEETARAAG, without attachment and hatred.

Practice Of Nonviolence

Our practice of nonviolence begins with the self. First, we should avoid mental and physical violence toward ourselves. Next, we should avoid violence toward our parents and other family members. Then we should avoid violence toward other human beings and animals. We should not commit one kind of violence to avoid another kind of violence. Here are a few simple rules to follow:

1. Even when things do not go as we wish, we should not get angry or upset.
2. We should be modest.
3. We should take only what we need. We should avoid waste.
4. We should be open-minded and fair. We should understand others' viewpoints. We should avoid things that may lead to violence. We should not do anything without giving it careful thought. We should not do things just because others do them.
5. We should not dislike people who do bad things. We should not take revenge. We should not do bad things ourselves.
6. We should not laugh at others' mistakes, clothes or appearance. We should keep in mind that

everybody makes mistakes.

7. We should keep our homes clean. We should keep our things in order. We should wear clean clothes.

8. We should trust that our parents always want the best for us. Their love for us is instinctive and unselfish. So we should try to understand their viewpoint and value their advice.

9. We should understand the importance of education. As students, studying and doing our best in school should be our primary goal.

10. When we get sick, we have bad feelings and thoughts. This is violence of self. So to maintain good health, we should eat healthy vegetarian food. We should rest and exercise properly.

11. We should remember that chastity, that is, purity of body and mind, helps us to avoid future problems.

12. We should not smoke, drink alcohol or abuse drugs. People become slaves of these habits. These things are also bad for our health. They limit our ability to think. People who use these things lose their sense of right and wrong. This is violence of self.

Four Views Of Bhagwaan Mahaveer's Life

by Sweta Shah[1]

Bhagwaan Mahaveer was born into a royal family. He was brave and fearless. As a child he could catch a snake and control an elephant. His real name was Vardhamaan, but because of these qualities, people called him Mahaveer, the brave one.

Moral: We should be brave and fearless. The only thing we should be scared of is doing bad deeds.

Mahaveer wanted to leave home and take the vows of a monk (DEEKSHA) at an early age. He asked the advice of his parents, King Siddharth and Queen Trishala, and of his elder brother, Nandivardhan. They were not happy with his becoming a monk at that early age. So Mahaveer waited until he was thirty years old and then he became a monk.

Moral: We should respect the feelings of our parents and other members of our family. We should not hurt their feelings by our actions.

---

1 Sweta, the daughter of Santosh and Bhavna Shah, wrote this article with the help of her parents at the age of eight.

Bhagwaan Mahaveer spent the first twelve years of monkhood in meditation, in the practice of nonviolence and self-control. Self-control means not having bad thoughts, anger, jealousy or hatred. Thus he got rid of four types of karma.[2] He made his soul very pure. He attained knowledge of everything. He became omniscient (KEVALI).

Moral: We should practice our religion so that ultimately we can remove all karmas from our souls. Then we will become happy forever.

Bhagwaan Mahaveer attained supreme spiritual knowledge (KEVAL JNAAN) at the age of forty-two. He devoted the next thirty years to teaching the principles of the Jain religion to others. One who attains supreme spiritual knowledge and teaches the principles of religion is called a TEERTHANKAR. Bhagwaan Mahaveer is our twenty-fourth TEERTHANKAR.

Moral: We should share our wealth of knowledge with others for the good of all.

---

2 These four karmas are knowledge-obscuring (JNAANAVARNI), perception-obscuring (DARSHANAAVARNI), deluding (MOHANEEYA) and obstructing (ANTARAAYA) karma.

How Does All That Happen?

Ketan: Daddy, the sun rises and sets. The moon shines at night. Wind blows and waves are formed on the surface of water. Sometimes it rains and sometimes it snows. There is lightning and thunder. How do these things happen?

Anuja: Ketan, my friend David once told me that God makes all these things happen. Daddy, is he right?

Father: Many people believe that God created this universe. They also believe that God does everything. However, Jainism says that the universe is eternal. All things of the universe have always been there in one form or another. Jains also believe that things happen on their own, on account of their natural qualities. Laws of nature make things happen.

Ketan: This concept is difficult for me to understand. Daddy, can you give me some examples?

Father: Let us understand how it rains. Water from lakes, rivers and oceans is turned into water vapor by the rays of the sun. Thus clouds are formed, and it rains.

Anuja: What about lightning and thunder?

Father: You know about electricity. There are two types of electric charge, positive and negative. When one cloud gets a large quantity of positive charge and another cloud gets negative charge, we see a huge spark going from one cloud to the other. Thus lightning and thunder occur.

Anuja: Can everything be explained in this manner?

Father: Modern science says that everything in nature occurs according to the laws of nature. Jains believe that everything happens on account of the properties (qualities) of matter, energy and souls.

Ketan: Daddy, how can properties of substances make things happen?

Father: Let me explain with an example. Sugar has the property of dissolving in water and sand does not have that quality.

Anuja: How do things happen in our lives?

Father: All worldly beings, animals, insects and plants, have souls living in their bodies. The important qualities of a soul are perception (ability to view and understand) and knowledge. These qualities of a soul are hidden on account of its association with matter. These factors affect the lives of all worldly beings.

Ketan: Daddy, does God affect our lives?

Father: Jains believe that when a soul becomes free from the bondage of matter (karmas), it becomes pure. Such pure souls are called SIDDHAS. A pure soul, SIDDHA, who has no likes or dislikes, no love or hatred, is God for Jains. Thus Jains do not believe that God (or SIDDHA) rewards or punishes us. We worship SIDDHAS as well as ARIHANTS as ideals to follow.

Anuja: I have heard that karmas affect our lives. What are karmas?

Father: There are two types of karmas, abstract (BHAAV) karmas and material (DRAVYA) karmas. Abstract karmas are our thoughts and feelings. These abstract karmas, our thoughts and feelings, cause very fine particles of matter to become attached to our souls. These particles are called material karmas.

Ketan: How do karmas affect our lives?

Father: The karma particles attached to our souls may affect our thoughts and feelings. They can also affect our bodies. When we have good thoughts and feelings, we are happy. On the other hand, if we have bad thoughts and feelings, we become unhappy. Thus our thoughts and feelings affect our lives.

Ketan: The things around us such as books, toys, school, teachers, friends and parents also affect our lives. Is it not true?

Father: Ketan, you are right. The things around us do affect our lives. In Jainism, these are called NOKARMA. They are not real karmas but seem to work like karmas. We should have good thoughts and feelings even when our karmas and NOKARMA are not favorable.

Anuja: Daddy, sometimes we feel pain. When we do not get what we want, we become unhappy. How can we be happy when bad things happen in our lives?

Father: Anuja, you are right. We do get upset when things don't go well. Still we should try to keep our cool when bad things happen to us. We should learn to face success and failure calmly. We should think carefully and do our best. We should understand that having bad thoughts is violence of self.

Ketan: Daddy, now I understand that it is important for us to make our lives better by having good thoughts and feelings and by doing good things. In this manner, we can also improve our NOKARMA – the things around us.

(15) God Will Give You More: A True Story

This is a true story related by Pandit Phool Chandra Jain Siddhantacharya.

Once Pandit Phool Chandra Jain Siddhantacharya went to buy some utensils for worship. The salesman showed him the utensils. Panditji selected some utensils and the salesman quoted the total price of the items. Panditji asked him to allow some discount.

The salesman said, "Brother, the utensils are for God's worship. Please do not bargain. God will give you more."

On hearing this, Panditji collected the utensils, put them in his bag and prepared to leave the shop.

On seeing this, the salesman said, "Wait a minute. How can you take the utensils without paying for them?"

Panditji said, "The utensils are for God's worship. Don't worry. He will give you a lot more."

The salesman realized his mistake and felt sorry. Panditji paid the bill and left.

Moral: We should not use religion as an excuse for getting money and material things.

Bhagwaan Mahaveer

by Duli Chandra Jain

Prince Vardhamaan, born in 599 B. C.,
son of Queen Trishala and King Siddharth,
kind, intelligent, fearless and brave,
earned the name of Mahaveer, a great hero.

Mahaveer saw that life's pain and suffering
are rooted in attachment, likes and dislikes.
So he left his princely comforts
to perform penance and meditation.

Mahaveer became an omniscient KEVALI,
he found the real nature of things.
He taught that real knowledge comes from
studying and accepting only what makes sense.

Mahaveer taught us to be independent,
not looking for favors from God or demigods.
He taught all living beings to help each other;
this is his message of nonviolence.

We pray to Bhagwaan Mahaveer
to learn the teaching of nonviolence,
to learn the teaching of self-help, and
to learn how to attain real happiness and peace.

How To Quench Hatred

A moral story from Buddhist literature

A long time ago, a king named Dighiti ruled over a small kingdom. He had a son named Dighavu. King Brahmadatt, who ruled over a neighboring kingdom, was more powerful than King Dighiti. King Brahmadatt attacked Dighiti, killed him and his wife, and took over his kingdom. Dighiti's son, Dighavu, escaped and went into hiding.

Dighavu decided to take revenge for the loss of his parents and their kingdom. But he had no means. So he took a modest job in the palace of King Brahmadatt. One night Dighavu was playing the flute and singing. King Brahmadatt heard the music and was very pleased by it. The next morning he called Dighavu, expressed appreciation for his talents, and appointed him his charioteer and companion. Dighavu was very happy. He saw an excellent opportunity for taking revenge.

One day, King Brahmadatt asked Dighavu to drive him to the forest in his chariot. The king enjoyed the trip. After a while, he felt tired and decided to take a nap under a tree. Dighavu saw a good opportunity to kill King Brahmadatt. When the king woke up, he told his charioteer, "I had a bad dream. I saw that my enemy

Dighiti's son is going to kill me." Just then Dighavu pushed Brahmadatt's head against the ground with one hand and drew his sword with the other. He revealed his true identity to King Brahmadatt. The king got scared and begged for his life.

For a moment, Dighavu thought that one stroke of the sword would kill Brahmadatt and his goal would be accomplished. Then he remembered that his father had taught him that hatred and violence only lead to more violence. Dighavu recalled his father's words: "Hatred is not quenched by hatred. Dear son, hatred is quenched by love." Dighavu had a change of heart. He said to King Brahmadatt, "I have the power to grant your majesty your life. Also, your majesty has the power to grant me my life." Dighavu put down the sword and let the king go free.

King Brahmadatt was moved by Dighavu's words. He embraced him and expressed his deep regret for what he had done to his family. King Brahmadatt returned Dighavu's kingdom and gave his daughter in marriage to King Dighavu.

After School

by Leona Smith Kremser

Two students are walking home together;
in fact, the hurried friend is a half-step
ahead of the gentle friend.

Rupa (hurriedly): You don't even answer;
don't you care what people say?

Neha (gently): Let them speak
from their own understanding.

Rupa: My father is rich. Perhaps,
he can help your poor father.

Neha: Thank you, but my father does
a decent honest job at a small college.

Rupa: My father gave the idol. What
did your father give for the new temple?

Neha: My father says our true gift is
to live our blessed Jain religion;
that is, to practice our five rules −
harmlessness, honesty, truthfulness,
purity, and freedom from attachment.

Rupa: Gold image!
O, how many bangles it would make!

Neha, you never go shopping!
Where do you go after school?

Neha (smiling): I go home.

Rupa (frowning): But home is so . . . busy;
mother with the club, brother with television.
What do you do at your home?

Neha: Well, I bathe;
then I help my mother prepare our prayer corner
for evening worship; then we talk.

Rupa: With your mother! Whatever about?

Neha: Well, my mother reviews my lessons,
or she tells me about our homeland;
the teaching nuns and the religious pilgrimages.
Of course, we prepare the evening meal
for father's homecoming before sundown.

Rupa: Our family prayer room remains dark,
my father decorates and lights it up for festivals.
(Slowly) Your prayer corner seems so . . enchanting;
sometimes, may I bring flowers?

Neha (gently): The Jain religion welcomes
all truth-seekers to the TEERTHANKAR'S feet.

Rupa and Neha: Blessed TEERTHANKAR.

The friends are now walking in step together.

Sanctum (VEDI) of Jain Temple
Dallas, Texas, U. S. A.

Jain Temple
Mombasa, Kenya

Jain Temple: An Ideal

Sheila: Grandma, last week, we had an interesting visit to our Jain temple.

Niket: Yes grandma, we really enjoyed the visit to the temple. There we saw two idols. One of the idols was decorated while the other one was plain. NAMOKAAR Mantra engraved on a tablet was placed between the two idols.

Sheila: Grandma, what is the difference between the two idols?

Grandma: There is no difference between the two idols. Both are images of VEETARAAG Bhagwaan. Both teach us the basic principles of Jainism. They teach us to avoid likes and dislikes. Both teach us to minimize anger, ego, deceit and greed.

Niket: If both idols represent the concept of VEETARAAG, then why is one of them plain while the other is decorated?

Grandma: Some people like a decorated idol while others like a plain one. Yet some others choose not to worship any idol at all. However, all Jains believe in NAMOKAAR Mantra.

Sheila: This is a good example of ANEKAANTAVAAD, our belief that truth has many sides.

Grandma: Sheila, you are right. We should not argue

about little things like different types of idols and different ways of worship. It is important to remember that we Jains indeed worship the concept of VEETARAAG. Moreover, we recite prayers and perform worships that remind us of the teachings of Jainism.

Niket: Grandma, I do not understand the meaning of most of the prayers and worships. Won't it be better if somebody explains their meanings when we go to the temple?

Grandma: Certainly, we need to learn the meanings of prayers and worships. We should also understand that rituals are not performed to obtain material things. Next time when we read a prayer, I will explain its meaning in detail.

Sheila: Grandma, I have seen some beautiful human figures in pictures of Jain temples. What are those? Do we worship them too?

Grandma: The male human figure is called YAKSHA and the female, YAKSHINI. There are some figures of angels as well. These figures are just decorations. We do not worship them. We worship only VEETARAAG. Some Jains do pray to imaginary guardian spirits called SHAASAN DEVS for favors. Seeking material favors is not proper. It is against the spirit of Jainism. A Jain temple teaches us to keep away from material desires.

Bharat And Bahubali

A Nonviolent Duel

By Kushal Raj Jain

Rishabhadev, also known as Adinath, was the first TEERTHANKAR of the present cycle of time. Bharat and Bahubali were two of Rishabhadev's sons. When Rishabhadev gave up his worldly possessions, he gave a portion of his kingdom to each of his sons. Bharat and Bahubali also received their shares.

Some years later, Bharat decided to become CHAKRAVARTI, a supreme ruler of the world. He asked all kings to accept his authority. Bahubali refused to do so. War was declared. The armies of both kings were facing each other. Their ministers thought that there would be bloodshed. Many soldiers would lose their lives. So the ministers advised that Bharat and Bahubali should engage in hand-to-hand combat. The two brothers agreed.

The first round was a water-duel between Bharat and Bahubali. Both stood knee-deep in a river and splashed each other with water. Bahubali won the first round. The second round was a sight-duel. The two brothers stood in the sun, staring at each other. The one who blinked his eyes first would lose the round. Again Bharat lost. The final round was wrestling. A huge crowd had gathered. The supporters of both were cheering. In the course of the duel, Bahubali managed to lift Bharat off the ground. He raised him high up in the air, whirling him around as he paced in the ring. Bahubali's supporters were happy and excited. Bahubali was going to be the supreme ruler of the world. At that moment, Bahubali realized that he was about to hurt and humiliate his own brother because of ego and pride. He thought, "Such pride is false. What good is it to become a king or the supreme ruler of the world? There is no end to such desires. Fulfilling one's desires can not lead to peace of mind." He gently put Bharat down, renounced his kingdom, and went in search of truth and peace.

* * * * * * *

There is perhaps no one of our natural passions so hard to subdue as pride. Beat it down, stifle it, mortify it as much as one pleases, it is still alive. Even if I could conceive that I had completely overcome it, I should probably be proud of my humility.

- Benjamin Franklin, in his autobiography

* * * * * * *

Places Of Pilgrimage

There are many places of pilgrimage in India for Jains. Sammed Shikhar, Shatrunjaya (Palitana), Mount Abu and Shravanbelgol are some of the most important ones.

Twenty-two TEERTHANKARS of the present cycle of time attained salvation (NIRVANA) at Sammed Shikhar. There are beautiful temples and CHARANS (representing the footprints of TEERTHANKARS). Sammed Shikhar is one of the most sacred places of pilgrimage for Jains.

There are thousands of beautiful temples on the hills at Shatrunjaya (Palitana). Therefore it is called the *City of Temples.* Most temples at Shatrunjaya have beautiful carvings in marble and stone. Shatrunjaya attracts visitors from all over the world.

Mount Abu is world-renowned for its Delwara Temples. These temples are located on high hills covered with palm trees. There are five temples at Mount Abu: Vimal Vasahi, Luna Vasahi, Pitalhar Temple, Khartar Vasahi and Temple of Mahaveer Swami.[1] These temples have been carved beautifully in marble and so they are called the hymns

---

1 In this context, Swami means virtuous and respectable.

in marble.

Shravanbelgol is near Mysore in South India. It is famous for the beautiful statue of Bahubali Swami, which is carved out of a mountain. The statue is about 60 feet tall. It reflects the supreme virtues of a VEETARAAG, one who does not have any likes and dislikes. Its message is that we should be humble and free from desires.

In Sanskrit, a place of pilgrimage is called TEERTH. It means ford, a place where one can cross a river. Great souls perform penance and meditation at solitary and peaceful places such as forests and mountain tops. They cross the ocean of worldly suffering and attain salvation. Therefore places like Sammed Shikhar and Shatrunjaya are called TEERTHS.

When we visit places of pilgrimage, we are reminded of the virtues of great souls who have become SIDDHAS. We tend to forget our everyday problems. We learn to have peace and happiness in life.

True Charity

by Kanti Mepani

Once upon a time, a businessman named Heeral lived with his family in a small town in India. He was very wealthy. He felt that the town had given him a good opportunity to conduct his business and so it was his duty to do something for the people of the town. He resolved to spend some of his wealth to help the poor people of the town.

Instead of giving away money, Heeral decided to distribute wheat. He decided to buy wheat at the lowest possible price so that as many needy people as possible could be helped. The wheat was of very poor quality, almost unsuitable for eating by man. Still the poor people gladly accepted whatever they were given. The distribution of wheat continued for some time.

One day, Heeral's daughter-in-law, Rashmi, saw the wheat that was being distributed. She was shocked to see what the poor were being offered. She respected her father-in-law so she did not say anything to him, but she still wanted to make her point.

Rashmi took some of the poor quality wheat, had it ground and made some chapatis (ROTIS or bread). She served those chapatis to her father-in-law. Heeral did not like the looks and taste of the chapatis. He asked Rashmi where she found the wheat for making those chapatis. She politely related the whole story. Heeral felt very sorry for what was being done under his direction.

In TATTVAARTH SUTRA, Acharya Umaswati writes: Charity depends on the kind of things that are given, the way the things are given, the thoughts of the giver and the nature of the recipient.

* * * * * * *

If instead of confining themselves purely to humanitarian work, such as education, medical services to the poor and the like, they (Christian missionaries) would use these activities of theirs for the purpose of proselytizing, I would certainly like them to withdraw.

- Mahatma Gandhi

Young India, April 23, 1931

* * * * * * *

Jain Yoga And Meditation

In Jainism, yoga means combined activities of body, speech and mind. Yoga consists of the thoughts we think, words we speak and actions we take. Clearly, all of us are always doing yoga. Depending upon our good or bad thoughts, speech and actions, we get good or bad karma. Therefore we should have good thoughts, use good words and do good deeds. We should practice good yoga.

Meditation means thinking about a given thing or event. Jainism teaches that there are four types of meditation. When we think about our loss or failure, we become sad. This is sorrowful meditation. When we are unhappy or angry with others, we wish that bad things would happen to them. This is inclement or unfavorable meditation. When we think of great souls and remember their virtues, we do righteous meditation. When a person becomes VEETARAAG, he or she performs spiritual meditation. It is good to avoid bad thoughts and feelings and do righteous meditation. We learn the real nature of things by performing righteous meditation.

Yoga and meditation help us with our practice of nonviolence. To avoid physical violence of self, we should keep our bodies healthy. For this we should keep a balanced vegetarian diet. We should do physical exercise to maintain our health. We should also take proper rest. To avoid mental violence of self, we should have pure thoughts and speak the truth. We should be nice to all. This way of living is true yoga and meditation. We should not do yoga and meditation as rituals. We should adopt yoga as a way of life.

* * * * * * *

Leave this chanting and singing and telling of beads!

Whom dost thou worship in this lonely dark corner of a temple with doors all shut?

Open thine eyes and see that thy God is not before thee!

Rabindranath   Tagore

Noble Laureate Indian Poet

* * * * * * *

The Spiritual Medicine

The Jain Theory of Karma In Action
by Rajeev Mehta[1]

Ajay: Grandma, grandma, I have a bad headache! May I have some aspirin or some other medicine?

Grandma: Well, Ajay, you are young. You eat healthy vegetarian food. You slept well last night. I am surprised that you have a headache. It seems to me that you do not need aspirin or any other medicine.

Ajay: Grandma, please give me some medicine. I am really suffering.

Grandma: Ajay, please be calm. Let us first figure out why you have this headache. Tell me what happened at school today.

(The doorbell rings.)

Ajay: That must be Sanjay.

Grandma: Why don't you go downstairs and help your brother bring in his books. I would like to talk with you both together.

(Ajay leaves. Later, he returns with Sanjay.)

Sanjay: NAMASTE, grandma.

Grandma: Sanjay, how was your day at school today?

Sanjay: Oh, the same as always.

Grandma: Do you have a lot of homework?

1 Son of Krishna Kumar and Chandra Mehta

Sanjay: I have three projects due tomorrow, but I finished them all yesterday. Today, I submitted them and got A's in all.

Grandma: Very good, Sanjay. I am happy for you. Now Ajay, tell me what happened in school today.

Ajay: Nothing, but I did not do very well on the science test and I got a C.

Grandma: Anything else?

Ajay: Nothing.

Grandma: It seems that you are trying to keep something from me. Please tell me what else happened. Speaking the truth is good for all.

Ajay: Well, I cheated on my math test.

(Grandma gasps in disbelief.)

Grandma: Didn't the teacher suspect you?

Ajay: When the teacher found out that cheating was going on and he looked at me, I lied to him.

Sanjay: What did you tell your teacher?

Ajay: I told him that Steve, who sits next to me, was cheating off me.

Grandma: I cannot believe that you would behave like that. Why did you bring up Steve's name?

Ajay: Steve is the top student in the class. I thought that if I told the teacher that he was cheating, the teacher would think that I was smarter than Steve.

Grandma: Do you understand what you have done? You cheated on the test and you lied. Moreover, you were jealous of Steve's success. No wonder you have a bad headache.

Sanjay: Grandma, how can lying, cheating and jealousy cause a headache?

Grandma: Everybody knows that lying or cheating is wrong. We commit violence of our own feelings when we lie or cheat. Similarly, thoughts like anger, jealousy and greed are part of violence. When we do such things, we have fear of getting caught. Such pressure can cause headaches and other diseases. According to the Jain theory of karma, these are bad karmas.

Sanjay: All religions teach that things like lying, cheating, greed and jealousy are bad. What is so special about the Jain theory of karma?

Grandma: The Jain theory of karma gives us freedom. It says that our thoughts and deeds make good and bad things happen in our lives. We do not do good things because of God's command. We do not do anything because of peer pressure. We do not depend on God for our well-being. Remember,

Our minds are for understanding good things.

Our eyes are for seeing good things.

Our ears are for hearing good things.

Our mouths are for saying good things.

25 Jainism: What Is The Difference? (Part 1)

Alpa: Ma, Jainism teaches us nonviolence and vegetarianism. It teaches us to speak the truth. It tells us that anger, pride, deception and greed are violence of self. Such behavior also leads to violence of others. Is there any religion that does not agree with these ideas?

Ma: Alpa, you are right. Teachings of all religions are similar to the Jain teachings. However, there is one important difference. Jains practice nonviolence to the greatest extent possible.

Alpa: Is there any other difference?

Ma: Jains believe that bad things like untruth, anger, pride and greed are forms of violence. We have to avoid such things to practice nonviolence.

Neel: Ma, if we lie or cheat, steal or hurt someone, we obtain bad karma. Our friends will not like us. These things are also against the law. Is that why we should not do bad things?

Ma: Yes! However, here is one more important point. It is proper to avoid bad things for fear of law or of bad karma, or peer pressure. However, it is best to avoid bad things because we want to lead a good clean life.

Alpa: What about fear of God?

Ma: Jains believe that God does not reward us or punish us. So the question does not arise.

Alpa: Ma, everybody is afraid of bad things happening to them. How can we face such things?

Ma: It is normal to have some fear. That is why followers of some religions perform rituals to seek the help of God. We Jains, on the other hand, regard that good and bad things are part of life. So we should face them calmly.

Neel: Ma, Jains also perform some rituals. We pray to TEERTHANKARS. We perform worship. Some Jains even pray to imaginary gods and goddesses. Do these things help?

Ma: Although people get some satisfaction by performing rituals, in fact, they can not prevent bad things from happening to us.

Alpa: But we do get some inspiration and confidence by doing such prayers and worship.

Ma: A better way to get inspiration, confidence and peace of mind is to understand that good and bad things will happen to us in our lives. We should carefully think and figure out what we should do in a given situation. Even if we do not succeed in spite of our best efforts, we should stay calm. This is part of our practice of nonviolence.

Neel: Now I understand that the Jain concept of nonviolence involves a lot more than not killing or hurting living beings.

Alpa: Ma, how can young children make proper choices?

Ma: Everybody makes decisions with the advice of family and friends. Young people should understand that parents have a selfless concern for their children's comfort and well-being. So children should trust their parents. They should seek and value their parents' advice. We should remember that hurting the feelings of one's parents is violence.

Neel: Should we always do things that our friends do or say?

Ma: It is helpful to listen to and follow one's good friends. However, we should understand that our friends do not have the same kind of feelings for us as our parents do. So it is better to seek our parents' guidance too. Blindly doing what others do is not proper. We should not yield to peer pressure.

Alpa and Neel: Ma, we now understand some special things about our religion of nonviolence.

26 The Story Of Agnibhuti And Vayubhuti

by Pandit Ugrasen Jain[1]

Once upon a time, there was a king named Atibal who was the ruler of Kaushambi. Som Sharma was his royal priest. Som Sharma and his wife Kashyapi had two sons named Agnibhuti and Vayubhuti. Som and Kashyapi loved their sons very much and tried to fulfill all their wishes. They did not discipline them properly. So Agnibhuti and Vayubhuti did not get much education.

Upon the death of Som Sharma, Agnibhuti and Vayubhuti were made royal priests by King Atibal. One day a scholar named Somil came to Kaushambi. Somil challenged Agnibhuti and Vayubhuti to a debate. They were defeated in the debate. So King Atibal dismissed Agnibhuti and Vayubhuti and made Somil the royal priest.

Agnibhuti and Vayubhuti became very unhappy. They felt sorry about missing the opportunity of getting an education during their school days. They decided to travel to some center of learning to study. Their mother, Kashyapi, suggested, "Dear sons, if you insist on going away from home for education, go to Rajagrah. My brother, Suryamitra, is the royal priest there. He is a great teacher. He will give you a good education."

Agnibhuti and Vayubhuti followed their mother's

1 Based on Jain Dharm Shikshavali by Pandit Ugrasen Jain, Part 2.

advice. They went to Rajagrah and related their story to their maternal uncle, Suryamitra. He listened carefully. He realized that his nephews had neglected their education because of the over-indulgence of their parents. Suryamitra thought that if he did the same, they would not learn much once again. So he told Agnibhuti and Vayubhuti that he did not have any sister and that he was not their uncle. However, if they wanted to get an education, he would teach them on one condition. They would have to support themselves. They would have to earn and learn.

Agnibhuti and Vayubhuti had no other alternative. They accepted Suryamitra's condition. They studied religiously and worked hard to earn their living. In due course, both became good scholars.

The time came for Agnibhuti and Vayubhuti to return to Kaushambi. They asked the permission of their teacher, Suryamitra. Suryamitra thought that it was time to reveal his true identity. He said, "Sons, I am pleased by your achievements. I am indeed your maternal uncle but I did not reveal this to you earlier. Perhaps, then you would not have learned much because of affection and indulgence. You might have missed another opportunity to get an education."

Suryamitra showered his nephews, Agnibhuti and Vayubhuti, with gifts and sent them back to Kaushambi. King Atibal was very impressed by the knowledge and scholarship of Agnibhuti and Vayubhuti, and reinstated them as the royal priests.

27 Jainism:
What Is The Difference? (Part 2)

Alpa: Ma, Jains believe that each soul is independent. Jainism teaches that self-help is the way to gain such independence. Jainism also says that the role of living beings is to help each other. Will you please explain these ideas?

Ma: Alpa, as you know, there are two kinds of souls: liberated souls (SIDDHAS), who have freed themselves from the bondage of karma, and worldly souls, who have physical bodies and the bondage of karma. All liberated souls are independent. The worldly souls are not completely free. Worldly beings live with the help of each other. They need food, water, air and other things. Depending upon their spiritual development, worldly souls enjoy varying degrees of freedom.

Alpa: Ma, worldly souls need many things to live. They need the help of other living beings. So they are not independent.

Ma: Alpa, you are right. I am happy to know that you understand that worldly souls are not completely independent.

Neel: Ma, in what sense are worldly souls independent?

Ma: Neel, let me explain this by means of an example. Suppose there are two classmates, Amit and Rekha. Both have the same teachers, books and other things. They depend on them for their studies. However, they are free to study as much as they want. They take the same test and both fail it. Amit stays calm and decides to try harder in the future. Rekha gets upset and blames everything in sight including her karma. In this respect, Amit and Rekha are free to do as they wish.

Alpa: Ma, this is a good example of our belief that truth is many-sided. Amit and Rekha are not free in some respects and yet they are free in other respects. This is called ANEKAANTAVAAD.

Neel: Ma, in this case, Rekha will get more bad karma than Amit.

Ma: Neel, you are right. The thoughts and feelings that we have in a given instance make our good or bad karma. You can see that Rekha's bad karmas are not going to help her in the future.

Alpa: Ma, I have heard that reciting some mantra can help us in examinations.

Ma: We can learn to be calm by understanding the meanings of prayers and mantras. However, a blind faith in the effect of mantras, prayers and worship may give us a false sense of security. So we may not study properly and fail the examinations.

Alpa: What is this way of thinking and understanding called?

Ma: Alpa, we can call it the rational way.

Neel: What is meant by rational?

Ma: Alpa, can you explain the meaning of the word 'rational'?

Alpa: Rational means based on reason. We see the things around us, study and discuss them. Then we accept only the things that appeal to our common sense. This is the rational way. Jainism teaches us to be rational. This is an important teaching of Jainism.

Neel: Some people believe in miracles. They tend to believe in things written in religious books or taught by religious leaders. Sometimes people accept traditional things. Sometimes people copy others. Is it proper to accept and do anything without thinking?

Ma: Believing in anything without giving it careful thought – not understanding things as one sees them, is delusion. Delusion is the root cause of many problems in life. A rational outlook, free from delusion, is the key to happiness and peace.

The Story of Bhagwaan Ram

This story is from the Jain religious book, PADMAPURAAN. A similar story appears in the religious books of Hindus as well.

A long time ago, King Dasharath was the ruler of Ayodhya. He had four sons, Ram, Lakshman, Bharat and Shatrughna. Ram's mother was Queen Kaushalya. Bharat was Queen Kaikeyi's son.

At the same time, King Janak ruled over Mithila. He had a daughter named Sita. Princess Sita was very beautiful. Just as Ram was wise and brave, Sita was intelligent and good-natured. King Janak arranged a SWAYAMVAR for Sita's marriage. SWAYAMVAR was a ceremony in which the bride would choose her own groom. King Janak invited princes from far and near. Ram and Lakshman were among those invited. The condition of SWAYAMVAR was that Sita would marry the prince who could handle the VAJRAVALI Bow. Of all the princes, only Ram could handle the heavy bow. Ram and Sita's marriage was celebrated with great pomp and show.

One day, King Dasharath decided to give up his throne and to spend his remaining days working towards spiritual enlightenment. He wanted to give the kingdom to Ram, his eldest son. However, some time ago, Bharat's mother, Queen Kaikeyi, had saved King Dasharath's life. So he had promised her three wishes. When Kaikeyi found out that Ram was going to get the throne, she reminded King Dasharath of his promise. She asked him to give the throne to her son Bharat and to exile Ram from the kingdom for fourteen years. King Dasharath agreed to fulfill his promise and renounced all his worldly possessions.

Ram was patient and understanding. He religiously followed the wishes of his father and left Ayodhya. His wife Sita and his brother Lakshman accompanied him. Prince Bharat was not in Ayodhya at that time. Upon his return, he found that his elder brother Ram had gone to live in the forest. Bharat felt very sad. He and his mother, Queen Kaikeyi, went to visit Ram. They tried to persuade Ram to return to Ayodhya. Ram would not go against the wishes of his father and politely refused.

Ram, Sita and Lakshman were content living in the forest. They helped several weak and needy people. One day, Sita was alone in the cottage. Raavan, the King of Lanka (Ceylon), saw her and was struck by her beauty. He took her to his kingdom against her wishes. When Ram and Lakshman returned to the cottage and did not find Sita there, they were extremely worried about her welfare. They set out to search for her. In the course of their search, they met Hanuman who joined them. Hanuman discovered that Sita was being held captive by Raavan in Lanka.

Raavan was a proud and powerful king. He wanted to marry Sita but not against her wishes. He had kept her captive in the hope that someday she would change her mind and agree to marry him. Raavan's brother, Vibheeshan, and his queen, Mandodari, tried to persuade him to release Sita but to no avail. Ultimately, Ram raised an army with the help of Hanuman. Ram invaded Lanka and Raavan was killed in the battle. Sita was freed.

After spending fourteen years in exile, Ram returned to Ayodhya. Bharat, who was taking care of the kingdom in his absence, returned the throne to Ram.

Ram was a benevolent king. He treated all people in his kingdom fairly. Everybody was happy. Later, Ram renounced his throne and became a monk. He performed penance, and finally attained salvation (NIRVANA).

The life of Ram is a glorious example for all, young and old. It teaches that we should respect our parents and be good to them. It tells us to love our brothers and sisters as Lakshman and Bharat did. The downfall of Raavan teaches us to be sensible. It teaches us that we should not be proud of our wealth and power.

Ram's life was as exemplary and perfect as can be. He was mindful of his duties. He was truthful and kind. He was brave and firm, free from anger and envy but he would not yield to injustice. Therefore, in Indian tradition, Ram is called MARYAADA-PURUSHOTTAM, the most ideal personality.